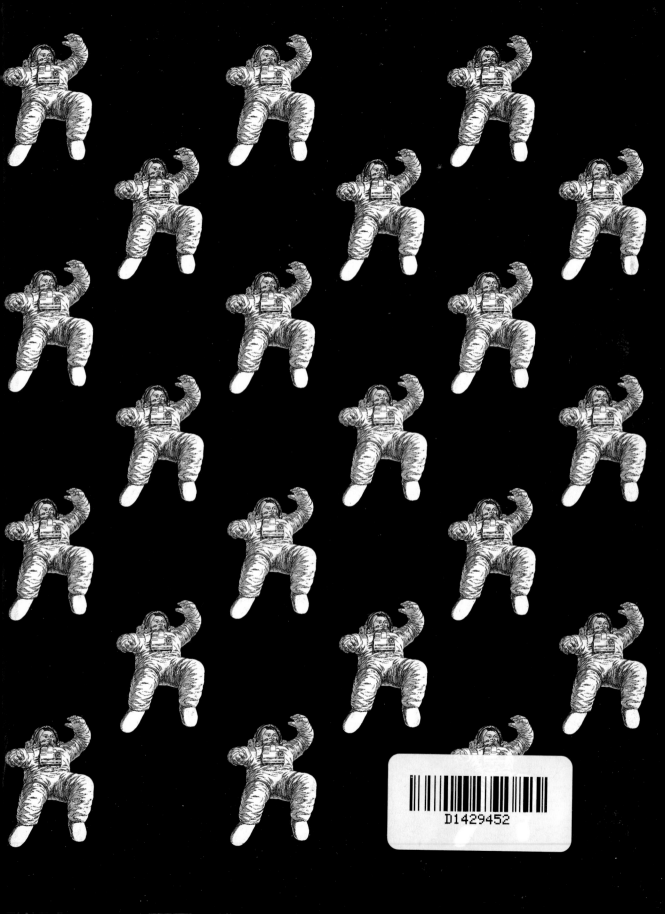

Thought this might help you
to get into your Space Suit!!

lots of love

Granma, Granpie
 xx   97

HOW TO SURVIVE

in outer
SPACE

Written by
Anita Ganeri
Illustrated by
Rob Shone

SIMON & SCHUSTER
YOUNG BOOKS

About the author:
Anita Ganeri has written and edited over 50 books for children, mainly on natural history and the natural world. She has travelled widely but has yet to travel into outer space.

About the consultants:
In 1991 **Helen Sharman** became Britain's first person in space, spending eight days on board Russia's MIR Space Station. A chemical engineer by profession, she spent 18 months in Star City, near Moscow, training for the Juno Mission. As well as lecturing and writing, she is currently presenting a science programme on TV.

Ian Graham has been interested in space flight since childhood and was present at Cape Canaveral for the first Space Shuttle launch in 1981. He is a Fellow of the British Interplanetary Society and a member of the American Institute of Aeronautics and Astronautics.

Copyright © S•W Books 1994

Designed and conceived by
S•W Books
28 Percy Street
London W1P 9FF

First published in Great Britain in 1994 by
Simon & Schuster Young Books
Campus 400
Maylands Avenue
Hemel Hempstead
Herts HP2 7EZ

Printed and bound in Belgium by
PROOST International Book Production

British Library Cataloguing in Publication Data available

ISBN 0 7500 1553 5
ISBN 0 7501 0783 9 (pb)

CONTENTS

INTRODUCTION

You've seen all the science fiction films, read all the books and even worn the T-shirt, but would you really be able to survive if you suddenly found yourself lost in outer space? How would you get into orbit in the first place? More importantly, how would you get back down to Earth? Don't panic! Your very own survival guide is at hand. To find out how to fly a space shuttle, get into a spacesuit in the correct order and rescue a wandering satellite, simply read on. Discover how to cope with weightlessness, space sickness and going to the toilet in zero gravity. And find out how the space travellers before you have managed it all...

WARNING! TRAVELLING IN SPACE CAN BE HAZARDOUS TO YOUR HEALTH. DON'T TRY IT WITHOUT A TRAINED ASTRONAUT (OR ALIEN) AS YOUR GUIDE.

WHERE IN THE UNIVERSE?

It's a big place, the Universe, and easy to get lost in. Before you set off on some serious space travel, try to get an idea of where you are and where you're heading. The Earth is one of nine planets in orbit around the Sun. Together with the asteroids, they form the Solar System. Until about 450 years ago, most people believed that the Earth was the centre of the Universe. In fact our entire Solar System is just a speck in outer space.

WHAT IS SPACE LIKE?

Outer space is dark and silent. There is no air to carry sound, so no one will hear you scream! The lack of air means that space is a vacuum, like the inside of a thermos flask but on a very grand scale. So grand, that distances are calculated in light years (the distance light travels in a year). One light year equals 9.5 million million km.

We are here

The Solar System contains nine planets in orbit around the Sun.

The galaxies, stars and planets formed from the hot gases scattered into space by the Big Bang.

The Universe is still expanding with the force of the Big Bang.

THE SOLAR SYSTEM

Nine planets orbit the Sun. Each also spins on its axis. The planets' moons and the asteroids complete the Solar System. Or do they? The search is on for a tenth planet beyond Pluto.

We are here

EXPLORER FACTS

Before the invention of space rockets, scientists used balloons to explore the atmosphere. At first, they travelled in the balloons themselves. But thin air above about 10km made breathing difficult, so unmanned balloons, carrying equipment were used.

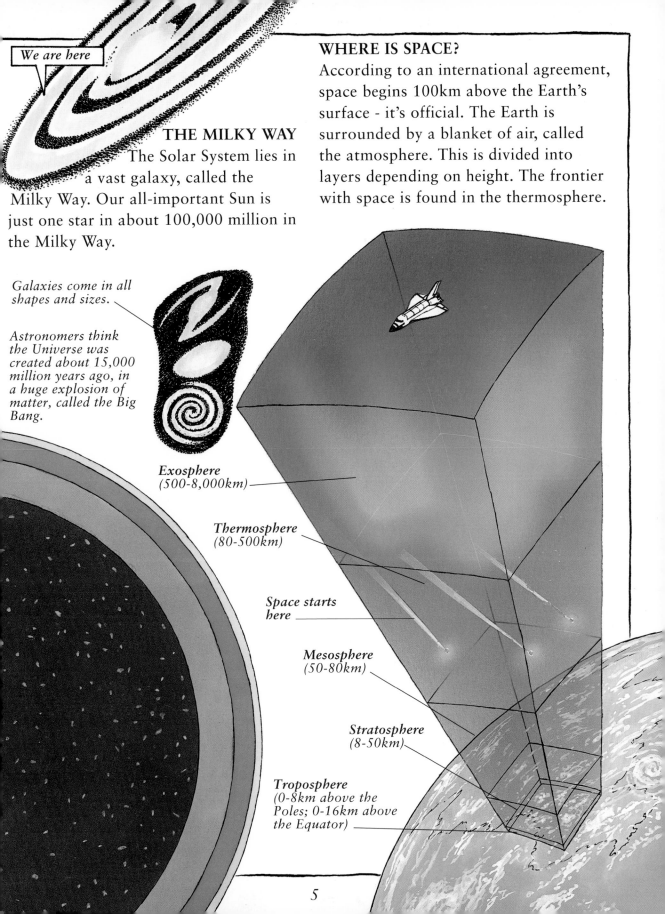

We are here

THE MILKY WAY

The Solar System lies in a vast galaxy, called the Milky Way. Our all-important Sun is just one star in about 100,000 million in the Milky Way.

Galaxies come in all shapes and sizes.

Astronomers think the Universe was created about 15,000 million years ago, in a huge explosion of matter, called the Big Bang.

WHERE IS SPACE?

According to an international agreement, space begins 100km above the Earth's surface - it's official. The Earth is surrounded by a blanket of air, called the atmosphere. This is divided into layers depending on height. The frontier with space is found in the thermosphere.

Exosphere (500-8,000km)

Thermosphere (80-500km)

Space starts here

Mesosphere (50-80km)

Stratosphere (8-50km)

Troposphere (0-8km above the Poles; 0-16km above the Equator)

SPACE SURVIVAL SUIT

You can't simply wander round space in the clothes you're standing up in. You need an air supply, for a start, and protection from the scorching heat of the Sun and bitter cold in the shade. On board your spacecraft, these aren't a problem but out in space proper, you need to wear specially designed gear. Don't worry if you find yourself floating upside down. In space, there's no right way up.

THE SPACE SUIT

Outside your spacecraft, you need to wear an 'extravehicular mobility unit', EMU, for short. The suit consists of three parts - the upper torso, lower torso (trousers) and the portable life-support system. It contains enough electricity and oxygen for seven hours (15 minutes to check your suit + six hours' activity + 15 minutes to take the suit off + 30 minutes in reserve). There is also a 30-minute emergency oxygen supply. The whole suit is made of layers of material, designed to protect your body from the radiation, heat or cold and keep it at the right pressure.

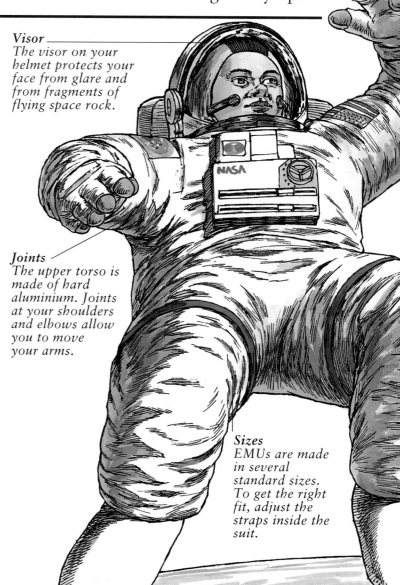

Visor
The visor on your helmet protects your face from glare and from fragments of flying space rock.

Joints
The upper torso is made of hard aluminium. Joints at your shoulders and elbows allow you to move your arms.

Sizes
EMUs are made in several standard sizes. To get the right fit, adjust the straps inside the suit.

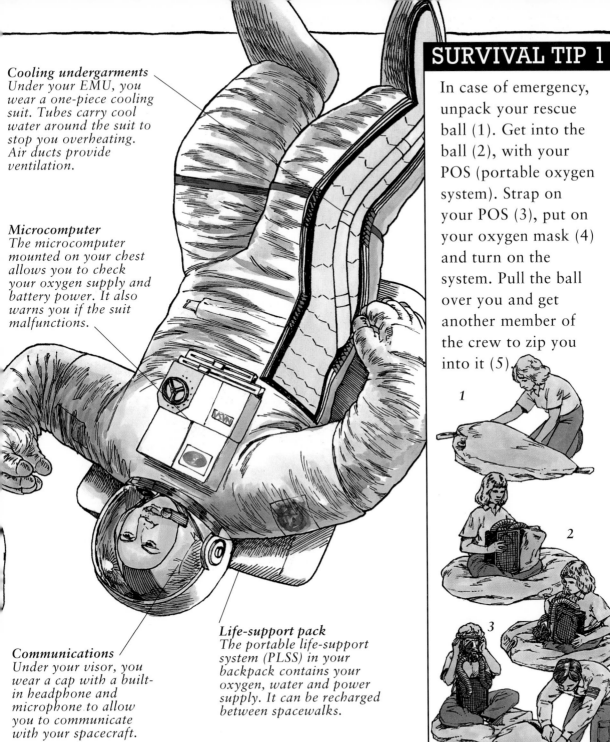

Cooling undergarments
Under your EMU, you wear a one-piece cooling suit. Tubes carry cool water around the suit to stop you overheating. Air ducts provide ventilation.

Microcomputer
The microcomputer mounted on your chest allows you to check your oxygen supply and battery power. It also warns you if the suit malfunctions.

Communications
Under your visor, you wear a cap with a built-in headphone and microphone to allow you to communicate with your spacecraft.

Life-support pack
The portable life-support system (PLSS) in your backpack contains your oxygen, water and power supply. It can be recharged between spacewalks.

SURVIVAL TIP 1

In case of emergency, unpack your rescue ball (1). Get into the ball (2), with your POS (portable oxygen system). Strap on your POS (3), put on your oxygen mask (4) and turn on the system. Pull the ball over you and get another member of the crew to zip you into it (5).

1

2

3

4

5

GETTING INTO YOUR SPACESUIT

With practice, it takes about five minutes to get into a space shuttle EMU. Put your suit on in a set order to avoid getting yourself in a muddle.

First, take some deep breaths of pure oxygen (1). Then put on your cooling and ventilation suit (2). Pull on your lower torso trousers (3), then reach your arms up into the upper torso (4). Now connect the water tube from your backpack to the tube in your cooling suit (5). Clip together the upper and lower halves of your suit (6).

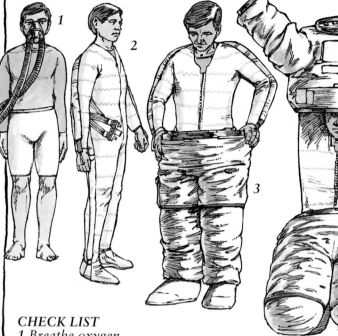

CHECK LIST
1 Breathe oxygen
2 Put on cooling garment 3 Put on lower torso
4 Put on upper torso 5 Connect water tube
6 Join suit halves 7 Put on communications hat
8 Put on gloves 9 Put on helmet

EXPLORER FACTS

The first living thing ever sent into space was a Russian dog, called Laika. She was launched in Sputnik 2 in 1957. The first person in space was cosmonaut, Yuri Gagarin.

John Glenn

Yuri Gagarin

On 12 April 1961, he orbited the Earth in his spacecraft, Vostok 1. In 1963, Valentina Tereshkova, became the first woman in space. The first American to orbit Earth was John Glenn in 1962.

Valentina Tereshkova

STARMAN OR SPACEMAN?

In the USA, people who go into space are called astronauts, and in the former USSR, cosmonauts. In fact, cosmonaut is more accurate. It comes from the ancient Greek word for the universe (kosmos) rather than just for star (astron).

EXPLORER FACTS

The first person to walk in space was the Soviet cosmonaut, Alexei Leonov, on 18 March 1965. He was connected to his spacecraft by an air hose. The first untethered space walk was made by an American, Bruce McCandless, in 1985.

6

7

8

9

Now put on your communications cap, or 'Snoopy hat' (7) and adjust the oxygen flow to your suit. Snap your gloves into place in your sleeves (8). Last but not least, put on your helmet (9). Check that everything is functioning and in position.

You are now ready to proceed out of the airlock and into space.

TRAINING TO BE AN ASTRONAUT

Of course, if you are really serious about surviving in space the best thing to do is enrol at astronaut training school. Here you will learn how to cope with all the stresses and strains of life in space. It's not going to be easy. Thousands of people apply every year to become astronauts and only a very few are chosen. But you might be one of the lucky ones...

G-FORCE TESTS

As part of training, astronauts are spun round at great speed in a centrifuge machine. This is to get them used to the high G-forces they will experience during launch. The normal G-force (pull of gravity) on your body is 1G. At take-off, it rises to 3G. This pushes you right back into your seat and makes you feel three times as heavy as usual.

UNDERWATER TRAINING

Once in orbit, the force of gravity does not affect you any more and you feel weightless. To help them get used to this feeling, astronauts spend a long time doing underwater training, in a huge tank.

ASTRONAUTS REQUIRED!

You need to be:

Calm and clear thinking

Able to give clear, concise information about what you are doing

Good at working with other crew members

Fit and healthy

One of the training aircaft is a modified Boeing 707. The effect it can have on the stomach has earned it the nickname 'vomit comet'!

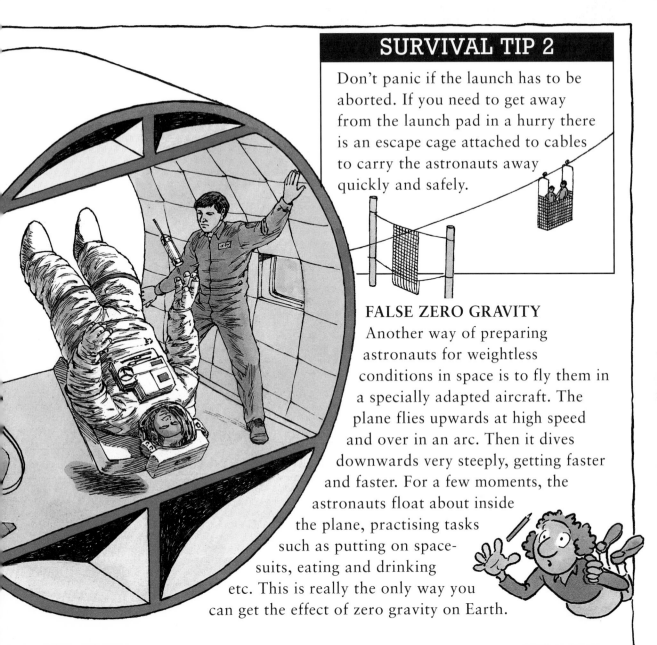

Don't panic if the launch has to be aborted. If you need to get away from the launch pad in a hurry there is an escape cage attached to cables to carry the astronauts away quickly and safely.

FALSE ZERO GRAVITY

Another way of preparing astronauts for weightless conditions in space is to fly them in a specially adapted aircraft. The plane flies upwards at high speed and over in an arc. Then it dives downwards very steeply, getting faster and faster. For a few moments, the astronauts float about inside the plane, practising tasks such as putting on space-suits, eating and drinking etc. This is really the only way you can get the effect of zero gravity on Earth.

EXPLORER FACTS

When the idea of sending humans into space was first considered, no one was sure what sort of people they should be. There was even the suggestion of sending up acrobats or tightrope walkers because they had a head for heights! In fact, the very first astronauts were highly skilled test pilots.

GETTING INTO ORBIT

You've completed your training with flying colours, and you are now ready for your first mission. But how do you get into orbit? Space may not sound very far away but you need an immensely powerful rocket to get you there. Astronauts, and many other satellites in low orbit around the Earth, typically travel at a staggering 8 km per second, which is nearly 29,000 km/h.

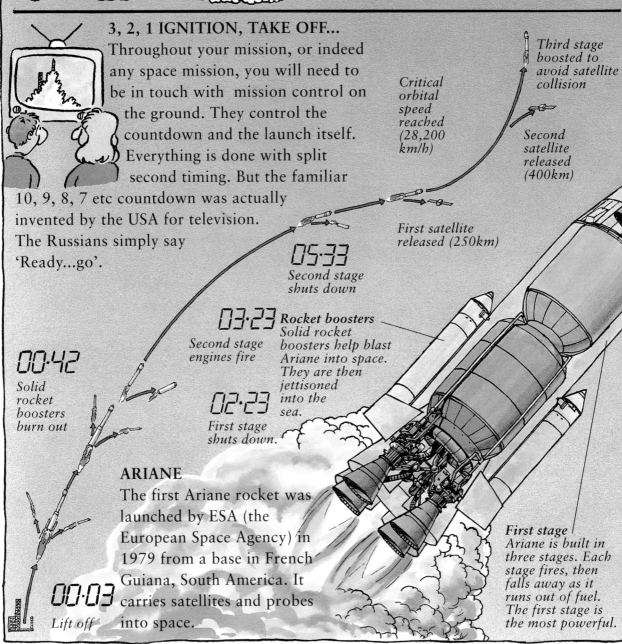

3, 2, 1 IGNITION, TAKE OFF...

Throughout your mission, or indeed any space mission, you will need to be in touch with mission control on the ground. They control the countdown and the launch itself. Everything is done with split second timing. But the familiar 10, 9, 8, 7 etc countdown was actually invented by the USA for television. The Russians simply say 'Ready...go'.

Third stage boosted to avoid satellite collision

Critical orbital speed reached (28,200 km/h)

Second satellite released (400km)

First satellite released (250km)

05·33
Second stage shuts down

03·23
Second stage engines fire

Rocket boosters
Solid rocket boosters help blast Ariane into space. They are then jettisoned into the sea.

00·42
Solid rocket boosters burn out

02·23
First stage shuts down.

ARIANE

The first Ariane rocket was launched by ESA (the European Space Agency) in 1979 from a base in French Guiana, South America. It carries satellites and probes into space.

00·03
Lift off

First stage
Ariane is built in three stages. Each stage fires, then falls away as it runs out of fuel. The first stage is the most powerful.

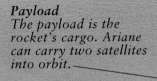

Payload
The payload is the rocket's cargo. Ariane can carry two satellites into orbit.

Third stage
The third stage engines continue to burn until Ariane is at its required orbit height.

Second stage
The second stage engines fire about three and a half minutes into Ariane's flight.

THE ROCKET ENGINE

Rocket engines are specially designed to work in the vacuum of space. Fuel needs oxygen to burn - a problem, given the lack of air in space. So rockets carry their own supply of oxygen, in liquid form. The fuel is burnt in a stream of oxygen. This produces gases which rush out through nozzles to boost the rocket along.

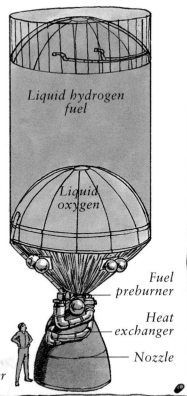

Liquid hydrogen fuel

Liquid oxygen

Fuel preburner

Heat exchanger

Nozzle

Rocket engineer

SPUTNIK TO SATURN V

Since they were first developed at the beginning of the 20th century, space rockets have got increasingly bigger and more powerful with each step. Some key rockets are shown below.

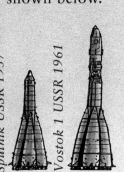

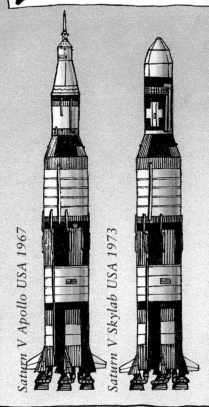

Sputnik USSR 1957

Vostok 1 USSR 1961

Soyuz USSR 1967

Saturn V Apollo USA 1967

Saturn V Skylab USA 1973

EXPLORER FACTS

The American physicist, Dr Robert Goddard, was one of the greatest space rocket pioneers. He launched the world's first liquid-fuelled rocket in 1926.

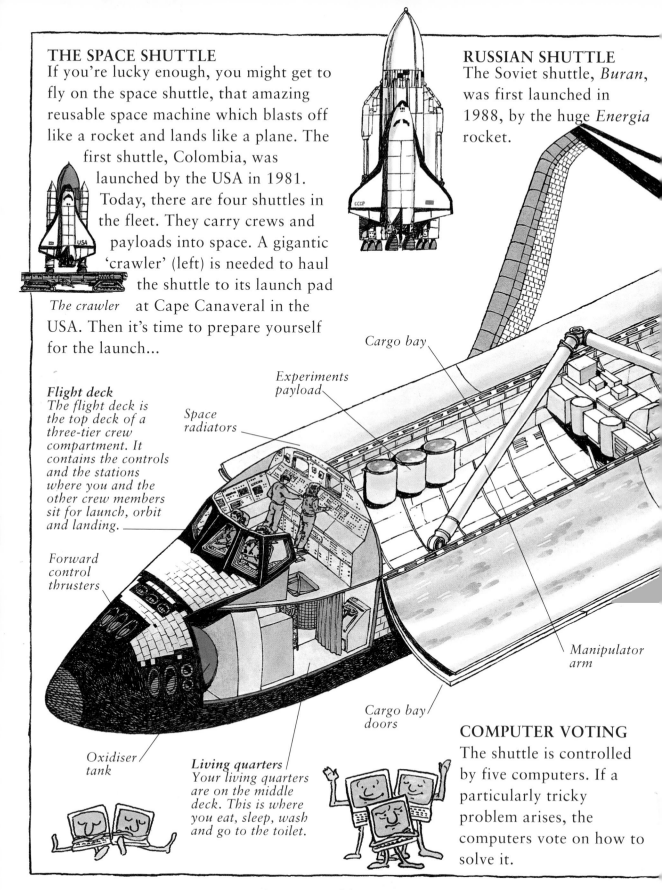

THE SPACE SHUTTLE

If you're lucky enough, you might get to fly on the space shuttle, that amazing reusable space machine which blasts off like a rocket and lands like a plane. The first shuttle, Colombia, was launched by the USA in 1981. Today, there are four shuttles in the fleet. They carry crews and payloads into space. A gigantic 'crawler' (left) is needed to haul the shuttle to its launch pad at Cape Canaveral in the USA. Then it's time to prepare yourself for the launch...

The crawler

RUSSIAN SHUTTLE

The Soviet shuttle, *Buran*, was first launched in 1988, by the huge *Energia* rocket.

Cargo bay

Experiments payload

Space radiators

Flight deck
The flight deck is the top deck of a three-tier crew compartment. It contains the controls and the stations where you and the other crew members sit for launch, orbit and landing.

Forward control thrusters

Manipulator arm

Oxidiser tank

Living quarters
Your living quarters are on the middle deck. This is where you eat, sleep, wash and go to the toilet.

Cargo bay doors

COMPUTER VOTING

The shuttle is controlled by five computers. If a particularly tricky problem arises, the computers vote on how to solve it.

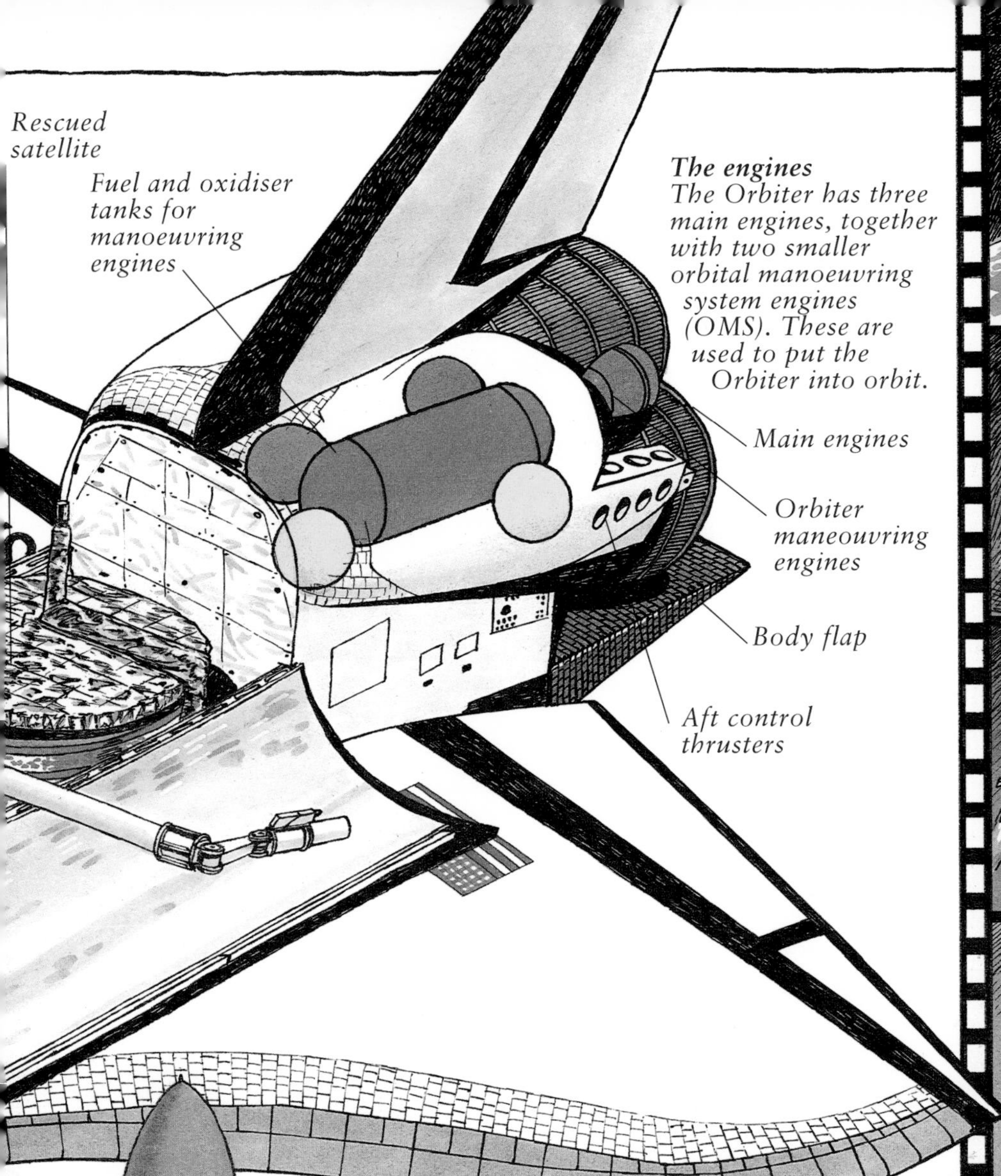

Rescued
satellite

Fuel and oxidiser
tanks for
manoeuvring
engines

The engines
*The Orbiter has three
main engines, together
with two smaller
orbital manoeuvring
system engines
(OMS). These are
used to put the
Orbiter into orbit.*

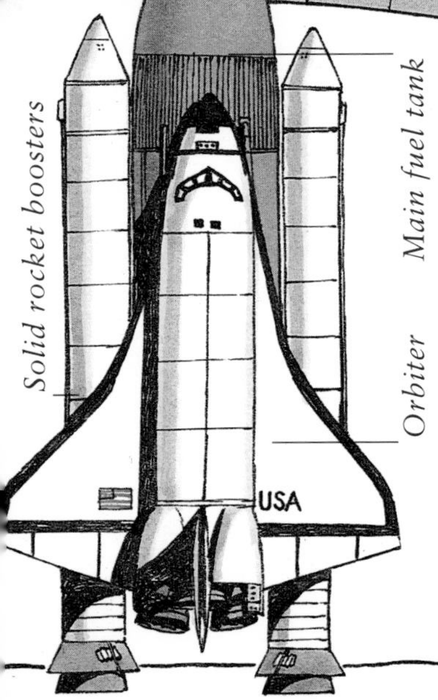

Main engines

Orbiter
maneouvring
engines

Body flap

Aft control
thrusters

Solid rocket boosters

Orbiter

Main fuel tank

USA

SPACE SHUTTLE BLAST OFF
The countdown is over and the space
shuttle blasts into space. The rockets
which fire it are as powerful as 30
jumbo jets. The reusable booster
rockets fall off and parachute back to
Earth. Then the main engines shut
down and the now empty fuel tank is
jettisoned. It breaks up on its way
down. The OMS engines fire to boost
the shuttle into orbit. You've finally
made it!

A TRIP TO THE MOON

Any astronaut-to-be dreams of a trip to the Moon. In 1969, the dream came true when the Apollo 11 astronauts landed on the Moon. When your turn comes, don't forget your spacesuit. There's no air on the Moon and gravity is a sixth of what it is on Earth. This makes golf easier (as Alan Shepard of Apollo 14 found out), but walking harder. It's much easier to bounce.

MAN ON THE MOON

The first manned Apollo mission to the Moon was launched by the USA in 1968. The USA and USSR had already sent up several unmanned probes. Between 1969-1972, 12 astronauts explored the Moon. Until that first famous step, however, no one was sure that it was even possible to land safely on the Moon.

Mission Control in Houston, Texas, USA

The Apollo Moon missions were carefully monitored by Mission Control in Houston, Texas, USA. It was not always plain sailing. During the Apollo 13 mission, the astronauts had to make an emergency return to Earth. An explosion had torn a hole in the side of their service module.

EXPLORER FACTS

On 20 July 1969, Neil Armstrong stepped on to the Sea of Tranquillity on the Moon. Billions of people heard his famous words, "That's one small step for a man, one giant leap for mankind!"

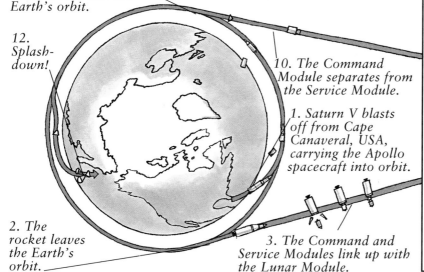

11. The Command Module re-enters the Earth's orbit.

12. Splash-down!

10. The Command Module separates from the Service Module.

1. Saturn V blasts off from Cape Canaveral, USA, carrying the Apollo spacecraft into orbit.

2. The rocket leaves the Earth's orbit.

3. The Command and Service Modules link up with the Lunar Module.

If you want to leave your mark on the Moon, a footstep or two will do. There's no air on the Moon so there's no wind or rain, or erosion. This means that footprints take millions of years to disappear.

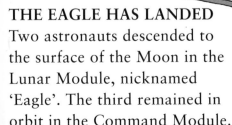

SATURN V

A new super-rocket was developed to launch the Apollo spacecraft, crew, equipment and all. This was Saturn V. It was built in three stages, with the spacecraft in the nose. At lift-off, Saturn V weighed almost 3,000 tonnes. Most of this was fuel. The rocket stood 111m tall.

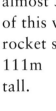

Launch escape system

Apollo Command Module

Apollo Service Module

Apollo Lunar Module

Third stage

Neil Armstrong on the Moon

Apollo Command Module

Apollo Lunar Module

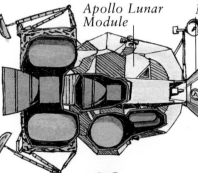

Second stage

Apollo Service Module

7. Its work done, the Lunar Module lifts off from the Moon.

4. The Apollo modules enter the Moon's orbit.

8. The Lunar Module docks with the Command Module.

5. The Lunar Module separates from the Command Module.

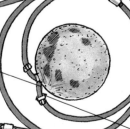

6. The Lunar Module lands on the Moon.

THE EAGLE HAS LANDED

Two astronauts descended to the surface of the Moon in the Lunar Module, nicknamed 'Eagle'. The third remained in orbit in the Command Module.

9. The Lunar Module is ditched. The Command and Service Modules leave the Moon's orbit and head for home.

First stage

STAYING UP THERE

Once you're in orbit, you need to maintain your high speed to stay up. There is no air in space, so there is no air resistance to slow you down. There are hundreds 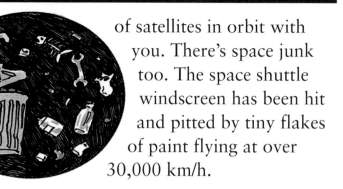 of satellites in orbit with you. There's space junk too. The space shuttle windscreen has been hit and pitted by tiny flakes of paint flying at over 30,000 km/h.

SELF-SUFFICIENT SATELLITE

Most satellites are blasted into orbit by unmanned rocket launchers. Many of the comsats (communications satellites) in space have been launched by Ariane. Once in orbit, satellites rely on solar panels to produce electricity to power their signalling systems.

They also use small rocket boosters to correct their movements if they wander slightly off course. Comsats are used to beam radio and television programmes, and telephone calls, around the world.

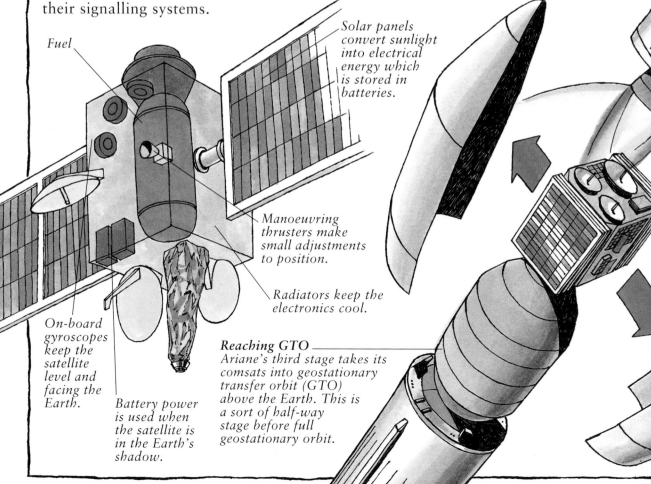

Fuel

Solar panels convert sunlight into electrical energy which is stored in batteries.

Manoeuvring thrusters make small adjustments to position.

Radiators keep the electronics cool.

On-board gyroscopes keep the satellite level and facing the Earth.

Battery power is used when the satellite is in the Earth's shadow.

Reaching GTO
Ariane's third stage takes its comsats into geostationary transfer orbit (GTO) above the Earth. This is a sort of half-way stage before full geostationary orbit.

18

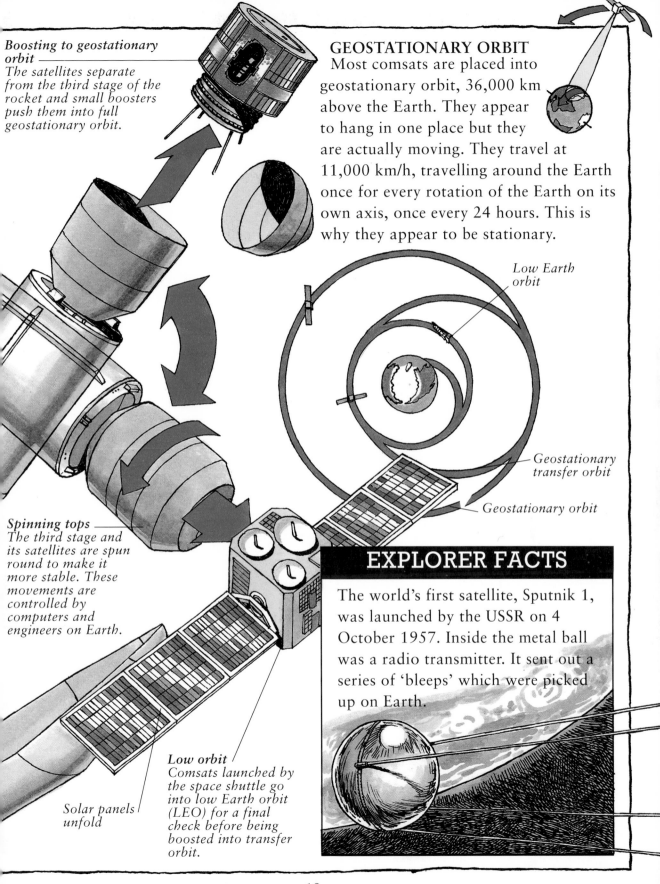

Boosting to geostationary orbit
The satellites separate from the third stage of the rocket and small boosters push them into full geostationary orbit.

GEOSTATIONARY ORBIT

Most comsats are placed into geostationary orbit, 36,000 km above the Earth. They appear to hang in one place but they are actually moving. They travel at 11,000 km/h, travelling around the Earth once for every rotation of the Earth on its own axis, once every 24 hours. This is why they appear to be stationary.

Low Earth orbit

Geostationary transfer orbit

Geostationary orbit

Spinning tops
The third stage and its satellites are spun round to make it more stable. These movements are controlled by computers and engineers on Earth.

EXPLORER FACTS

The world's first satellite, Sputnik 1, was launched by the USSR on 4 October 1957. Inside the metal ball was a radio transmitter. It sent out a series of 'bleeps' which were picked up on Earth.

Solar panels unfold

Low orbit
Comsats launched by the space shuttle go into low Earth orbit (LEO) for a final check before being boosted into transfer orbit.

LIVING IN SPACE

How do you think you'll cope with living and working in space? The strangest feeling to get used to is that of weightlessness. Being able to float around inside your spacecraft might be good fun at first, but it can get a bit trying if you want to have a bite to eat or conduct an experiment. You'll get used to it in a couple of days. In the meantime, happy floating!

SPACE STATIONS

Space stations were designed so that astronauts could live and work in space for weeks and even months on end. The first space station, Salyut, was launched by the USSR in 1971. It was followed by the USA's Skylab in 1973. The new Soviet space station, Mir, (right) went into orbit in 1986. A large number of Soviet and guest cosmonauts (including this book's consultant) have visited Mir.

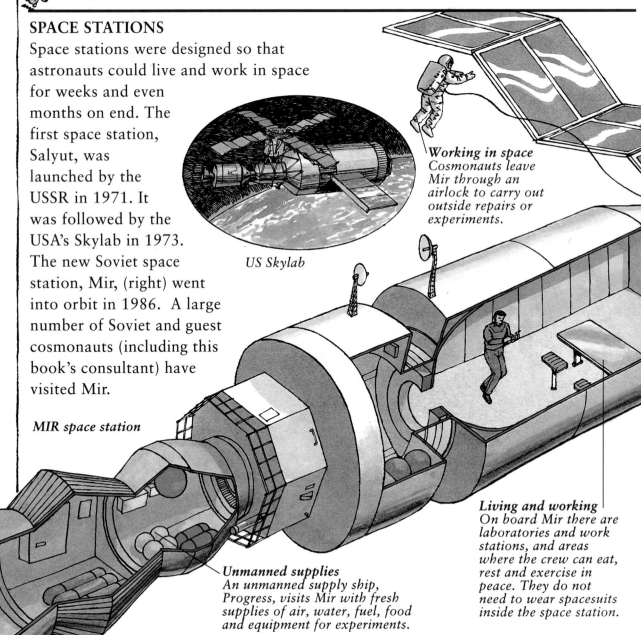

US Skylab

Working in space
Cosmonauts leave Mir through an airlock to carry out outside repairs or experiments.

***MIR** space station*

Unmanned supplies
An unmanned supply ship, Progress, visits Mir with fresh supplies of air, water, fuel, food and equipment for experiments.

Living and working
On board Mir there are laboratories and work stations, and areas where the crew can eat, rest and exercise in peace. They do not need to wear spacesuits inside the space station.

The longest time spent in space is a year and a day. The record is held by two Mir cosmonauts, Vladmimir Titov and Musa Manarov.

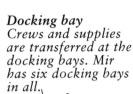

ADAPTING TO SPACE

One of the main reasons for building the space stations was to see how people (and other living things) adapt and get used to the strange conditions in space, such as weightlessness. Space station astronauts monitor themselves to see how their blood pressure and heart rates are affected. They have also tested the effect of weightlessness on spiders, fish, monkeys and frogs. Spiders on Skylab still managed to spin their webs normally. It was also possible to grow normal plants.

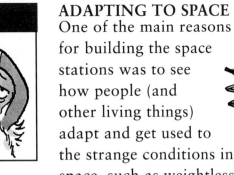

Docking bay
Crews and supplies are transferred at the docking bays. Mir has six docking bays in all.

New crews
The new cosmonauts arrive on the space ferry, Soyuz. It can carry two to three people.

Power from the Sun
Mir gets most of the energy it needs to power its equipment from the Sun.

Energy from the Sun

Negative silicon layer

Positive silicon layer

Solar panels
Mir has fold-out solar panels which trap the Sun's energy falling on them and convert it into electricity. Sunlight triggers off a flow of electrons in the silicon cells, creating an electric current.

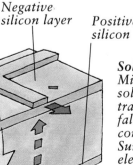

SURVIVAL TIP 4

For the first few days in space, you may feel slightly dizzy and sick. Don't worry - it's a simple case of space sickness. On the shuttle, you wear a medicated patch behind one ear. It stops you feeling sick.

ON BOARD THE SHUTTLE

Living conditions on the shuttle, weightlessness apart, are made as close as possible to those on Earth. Air and water are supplied to the crew compartment (right) by the shuttle's life-support system.

Whatever your job on board the space shuttle, as pilot, commander or payload specialist, there are certain things you must do. To prevent your heart and other muscles getting weaker in the zero gravity, you must take plenty of exercise. You are also given plenty of rest - eight hours are set aside for sleep.

You have 45 minutes to get ready for bed. You sleep in bunks, strapped into sleeping bags. One bunk is upright but in space it doesn't matter if you sleep standing up. In the morning, you have 45 minutes to get washed and ready for work. A shower isn't possible - you have to make do with a wet washcloth instead.

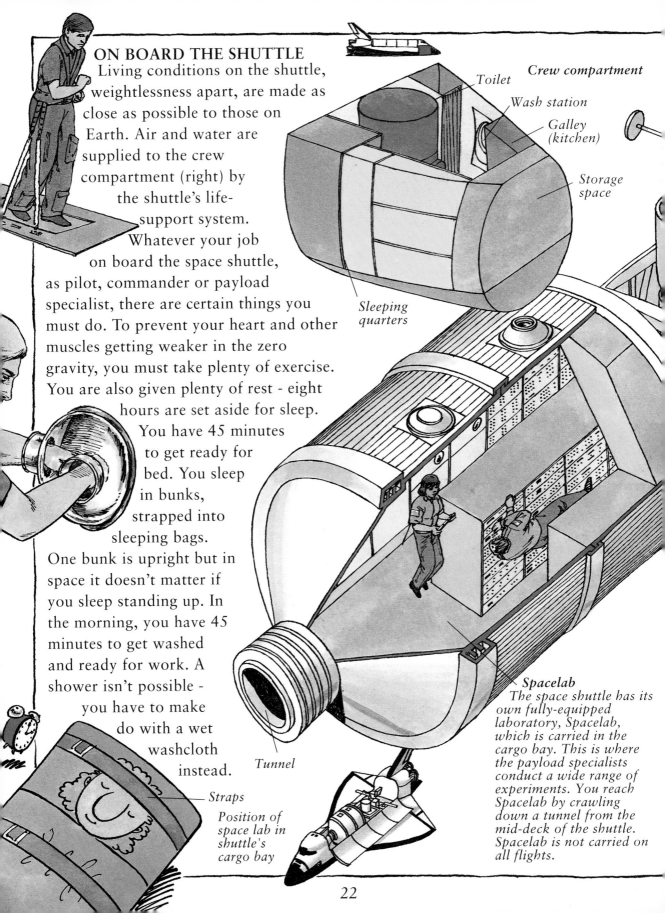

Crew compartment

Toilet

Wash station

Galley (kitchen)

Storage space

Sleeping quarters

Tunnel

Straps

Position of space lab in shuttle's cargo bay

Spacelab
The space shuttle has its own fully-equipped laboratory, Spacelab, which is carried in the cargo bay. This is where the payload specialists conduct a wide range of experiments. You reach Spacelab by crawling down a tunnel from the mid-deck of the shuttle. Spacelab is not carried on all flights.

Pallet segments
Another part of Spacelab is the pallet segments. These are exposed to space. They carry scientific instruments, such as telescopes, for outside experiments.

Working outside

SURVIVAL TIP 6

When you've got to go, you've got to go but the space shuttle toilet may take a bit of getting used to. Waste can't be flushed away with water. It has to be sucked away by air. As part of your preparation for your flight, study the diagram below. It'll save time later!

Odour filter

Commode operating handle

Control panel

Waist restraint
Seat
Urinal
Foot control

Experiments
A great many experiments are carried out aboard the shuttle. Astronauts investigate living things, materials and ways of looking at space.

SURVIVAL TIP 5

On board the shuttle, you wear comfortable, blue cotton overalls. They have plenty of pockets for holding essential items such as sunglasses, pens, torch, penknife and scissors. These are attached with Velcro to stop them flying off.

Torch

Sun-glasses

Pencils and pens

Penknife

Scissors

EATING IN SPACE

Gone (almost) are the days of sucking your lunch out of a toothpaste tube! Your meals arrive on a personally-coded tray. Just stick your tray in the microwave (situated above the food trays). When ready, open your food packages (this is where your scissors come in handy) and tuck in.

Microwave

Supper on the shuttle
Shrimp cocktail
Beef steak
Rice
Broccoli in cheese sauce
Fruit cocktail
Butterscotch pudding
Grape juice

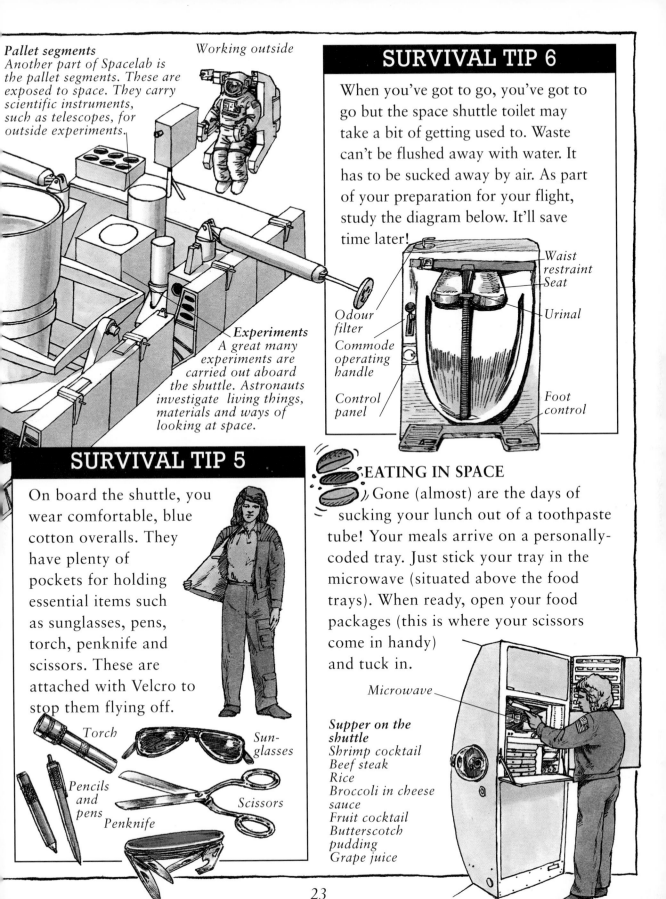

RESCUING A SATELLITE

As an intrepid shuttle astronaut, rescuing or repairing a faulty satellite may just be part of your normal working day. It's a dangerous job, of course, but someone's got to do it! In 1992, three shuttle astronauts spent eight hours on a space walk to rescue the huge comsat, Intelsat 6. They finally managed to haul it into the shuttle's cargo bay, fitted it with a new rocket motor and sent it back into orbit.

EVA

Rescuing a satellite is going to involve you in a spot of EVA (extra-vehicular activity). Astronauts used to be tethered to their spacecraft by a long hose which supplied them with air. Now they use an MMU.

The MMU
The Manned Manoeuvring Unit (MMU) latches on to your EMU spacesuit so that it looks as if you're sitting in a very high-tech armchair. It is powered by 24 jets of nitrogen gas which can be fired to move you in any direction you want to go.

Video camera
A battery-powered video camera mounted on the MMU can send pictures back to Earth via the shuttle.

Roll — Button — Pitch — Yaw

Controls
The MMU's flight controls are in the ends of the arm rests. Use the left-hand control to move in a straight line. Use the right-hand control to pitch up or down, yaw left or right or to turn round.

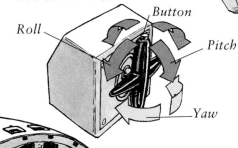

Airlock

GETTING OUT

MMU Before you can walk anywhere, you have to get out of the shuttle. You leave through a small room, called the airlock. You put on your MMU in the cargo bay.

REMOTE MANIPULATOR ARM

A mechanical arm is used to move payloads in and out of the shuttle's cargo bay. It is called the Remote Manipulator System (RMS). The arm has joints at the shoulder, elbow and wrist, and TV cameras so the person operating it can check its movements. The 'hand' has three wires which grip on to a payload and hold it tight.

TV camera

Wrist joint

Snare wires

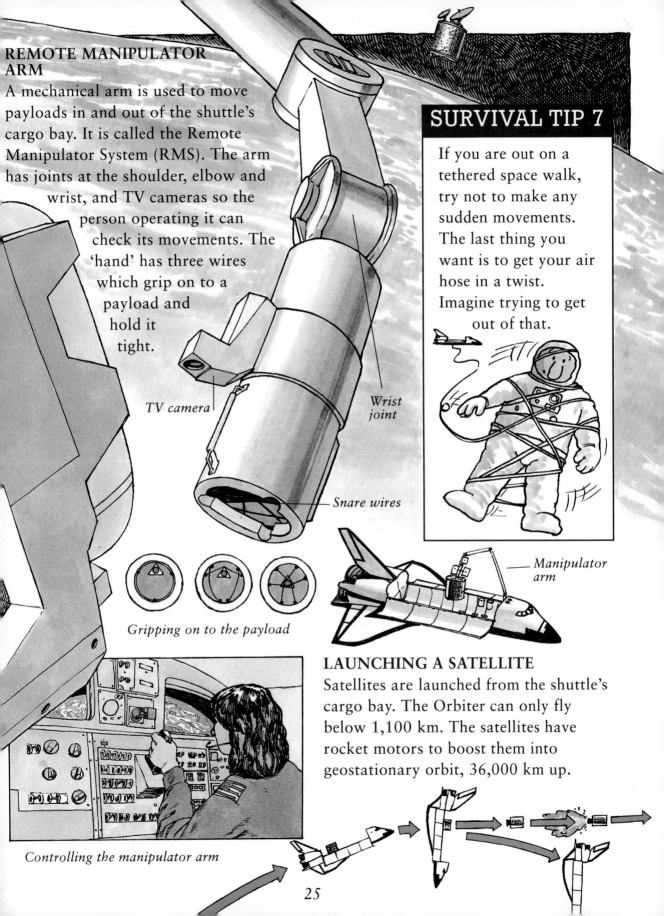

Gripping on to the payload

Controlling the manipulator arm

SURVIVAL TIP 7

If you are out on a tethered space walk, try not to make any sudden movements. The last thing you want is to get your air hose in a twist. Imagine trying to get out of that.

Manipulator arm

LAUNCHING A SATELLITE

Satellites are launched from the shuttle's cargo bay. The Orbiter can only fly below 1,100 km. The satellites have rocket motors to boost them into geostationary orbit, 36,000 km up.

ARE WE ALONE?

The search for aliens is on - it's official! SETI (the Search for Extraterrestrial Intelligence) has been set up to find life in other parts of the Universe. It may not find another E.T., but a runaway Martian would be a start. As far as we can tell, Earth is the only inhabited place in the Universe (at least, in our Solar System). But we may be wrong. So, keep your eyes peeled.

Deep space camera
Voyager 2 beamed back spectacular pictures of the planets using its highly sophisticated imaging systems.

PROBING THE PLANETS

Unmanned planetary probes have been sent into space for the last 30 years. Their mission - to explore and photograph the planets. Some have ventured further into outer space, carrying messages for any aliens they might encounter. The two Pioneer probes carry plaques (below), showing the Earth's position in space and a man and woman. The Voyager probes (right) have long-playing records on board, with music and greetings from different parts of the Earth, together with snippets of bird and whale song.

Venus probe

VOYAGER 2

Launched in 1977, Voyager 2 flew past Uranus in 1986 and Neptune in 1989 before leaving the Solar System for ever. It was the first probe to visit these two planets. Its journey lasted 12 years and covered 6 billion km.

People have watched the skies for thousands of years. Until 1609 they had to rely on their eyesight alone. Then Galileo set the trend of using the newly invented telescope.

Radio signals
This large dish is an aerial for picking up radio signals coming from Earth. The signals instructed the probe what to do.

VIKING LANDER

In 1976, two Viking probes landed on Mars. They took amazing pictures of Mars' dusty, red surface and samples of its soil. But they found no signs of life.

LOOKING AND LISTENING

In 1990, the Hubble space telescope was launched from the space shuttle. It has already sent back pictures of quasars and gas bubbles from stars, never seen before. But, a

slight technical hitch with one of the mirrors means they were rather fuzzy. A repair mission in December 1993 has

Hubble space telescope

fixed it. If any aliens do try to make contact, their messages may be picked up by gigantic radio telescopes on Earth. These also send messages into space.

Nuclear power
At the edge of the Solar System, the Sun's energy is too weak to use as solar power. Voyager's nuclear powerpacks produce its electricity.

Radio telescope

GETTING BACK DOWN TO EARTH

You've reached for the stars, rescued a satellite and narrowly missed meeting a Martian, but now it's time to head back to Earth. Unmanned satellites fall back to Earth and burn up as they re-enter the Earth's atmosphere. But, with people aboard, it's not that simple. So, strap yourself into your seat and brace yourself for landing. You'll soon have your feet firmly back on the ground.

RE-ENTRY

The space shuttle lands on an ordinary Earth runway, like an ordinary Earth glider (see below). Other re-entries are rather bumpier. When Yuri Gagarin made his historic flight in 1961, his capsule re-entered the Earth's atmosphere at 20 times the speed of sound. As it plummeted towards the ground, Gagarin had to bail out and parachute to Earth. The Apollo astronauts splashed down in the ocean, inside their spacecraft. It had parachutes to slow its landing. They were then rescued by boat. The Russians still land on dry land, using parachutes and retro rockets. One of the major problems of re-entry is the intense heat created as the spacecraft reaches the Earth's atmosphere. Heatshields are used to absorb or deflect heat. The space shuttle is covered with tiles which can survive temperatures up to 1,400°C.

SPACE SHUTTLE LANDING

1 To land the shuttle, turn the Orbiter round so it is flying tail first. Fire the OMS engines to reduce your speed.

2 Then turn the Orbiter the right way round again and raise its nose. You will begin to lose height as you slow down.

3 You start re-entry at a height of 122km. The intense heat generated causes a communications blackout for 12 minutes.

It takes years of training to understand the thousands of switches on the shuttle's flight deck. You have plenty of time to practise on the SMS (Shuttle Mission Simulator) before you are let loose on the real thing. Even then, for most of the flight, the computers are in control. The key controls are shown below.

1 Seat
2 Helmet
3 Joystick
4 Computer keyboard
5 Visual display unit
6 Attitude direction indicator
7 Auto pilot
8 Cabin air conditioning
9 Atmospheric control
10 Landing gear
11 Abort button
12 General purpose computer switches

4

4 During this time, you control your descent by a series of manoeuvres called S-turns.

5 Finally, you glide in to land on the runway. Your mission is over.

THE FUTURE IN SPACE

Your next journey into space might be a mission to Mars. The Americans are looking at the possibility of such a project and of putting a permanently-manned space station (Freedom) into orbit by the year 2000. In the 21st century, living and working in space might be everyday events. Holiday brochures might include inter-galactic spacebus tours, or activity weekends on the Moon. Who knows?

MINING THE ASTEROIDS

In future, as the Earth's resources run out, mining the asteroids might be the answer. Robots could be used to survey likely asteroids. Then spaceships could tow them into orbit around the Earth. A mining base could also be set up on the Moon. Miners and their families would live permanently on the Moon in a special lunar base.

LIVING IN THE CITY

One plan for easing the overcrowding on Earth is to build huge, wheel-shaped cities in space. Conditions inside the cities would be made as close as possible to conditions on Earth, with fields, shops, houses, offices and so on. The city would be built from moon rock.

BIOSPHERE II

To survive on Mars, people would have to live in a sealed greenhouse, called a biosphere, with its own water, air and food supply. A prototype was built in the USA to see if such a colony would work. Eight volunteers spent two years sealed inside.

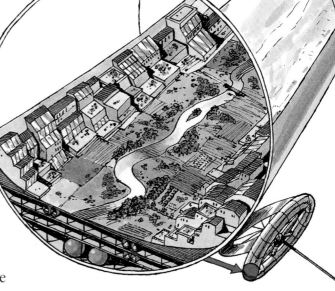

GLOSSARY

Airlock A small room in a spacecraft where an astronaut prepares to go out of the craft into space.

Air resistance The way in which air slows an object down. This is why ordinary aircraft need powerful engines to keep them moving.

Asteroid A lump of space rock or metal travelling in the asteroid belt between the planets Mars and Jupiter.

Astronomer A person who studies objects in space.

Axis An imaginary line drawn through a planet from top to bottom. The planet spins around its axis.

Erosion The wearing away of the land by wind and rain for example.

Galaxy A huge group of stars.

G-force The force on your body relative to gravity.

Gravity An invisible force which pulls objects downwards or towards each other. The pull of the Earth's gravity is what keeps your feet on the ground and brings a ball down again if you throw it up into the air.

Jettisoned Thrown off or overboard.

Orbit The curved path taken by one object as it travels around another object in space.

Payload A spacecraft's cargo, for example, a satellite or probe.

Satellite A natural or man-made object which orbits another object in space.

Universe Space and everything in it.

Vacuum An area which contains nothing at all, not even air.

Weightlessness In space, you may feel as if you have no weight because you are not affected by gravity as you are on Earth.

INDEX